A Short Stretch of the Legs

My Penny Mile Camino

Carol Ann Creagh

www.selfpublishbooks.ie

A Short Stretch of the Legs. My Penny Mile Camino.

ISBN 978-1-910097-15-1 Paperback

ISBN 978-1-910097-20-5 Hardback

Front cover design: Michael Creagh

Published and printed in Ireland by Lettertec Ireland Ltd.

Contents

To my Wonderful Dad

I will love you always and miss you forever

Preface

A quick glance at the calendar, only forty days before I put my size three and a half feet onto the first mile of the Camino de Santiago de Compostela – a 500 mile pilgrimage across northern Spain.

'Why?' you might ask… Answer is 'why not?'

I have a choice, live life sitting on my hands or lacing up my trainers and head off on the adventure of a lifetime. And anyone who knows me knows that my hands are never to be found under my butt. As for my feet, they are only happy when they are trekking through the dust of Africa or the dampness of Asia. Well, now it is Europe's turn.

I happened upon the Camino purely by chance, though I don't think anything in life is chance… Climbing Cavehill feeling quite lost following the death of my beloved dad, I met two girls training for the Camino. The following day meeting another friend on the same hill, he started talking about his Camino. Finally, that evening an e-mail from a third friend said how I should consider the Camino to help me through my grief. Signs were everywhere!

Within three weeks I was on my way to walk half the Camino; 220 miles in 10 days from Leon to Santiago, but reaching the cobbles in front of the Cathedral surrounded by those pilgrims who had started in France weeks or months earlier I felt I had cheated…

Halfway was not enough. I knew I would have to return to walk the entire "Way of St James".

1

Lost

'Lost' is a very small word with such a big meaning. I constantly lose things – car keys, mobile phone, the TV remote… But these are OK as they usually turn up down the side of couches or secreted deep in jacket pockets, but to lose people, that's very different. This loss has no end, a dark forever stretching in front of you, a tunnel of emptiness… Returned from Greece with my book *"Angels under my Bed"* completed and a suntan for my trouble, my first stop was to look in on my dad. Cancer was now destroying the body of this great man, but his courage and determination kept him going through his pain. He was in good spirits but fading fast in front of my eyes. District nurses were now supplying walking aids and wheelchairs. Indignation to a man whose feet owned the Belfast hills…

I can still hear his rhythmic pace beating the ground as I skipped beside him, my feet taking three steps to his one. Shoe, shoe, stick, shoe, shoe, stick… His blackthorn tapping the ground with a reassurance it knew where it was taking us. Multitasking, it would swish nettles away before contact with my small ankle socked legs, it would fiend off dogs who ventured too close and on several occasions it felt its way for us as the mist enveloped us on the nose of McArt's Fort. Beside him childhood Sundays were spent climbing the hills that hugged Belfast. Our home, though in the city, was surrounded by beautiful greenery. The soft curve of the Black Mountain bade me good morning outside my bedroom window and quietly whispered goodnight, as its TV mast perched on its ridge, flickered red lights into my dreams. The dark green landscape stretching into Divis, protecting the west, Cavehill, protecting the north, and across the narrow strip of river Lagan the not so dominant Craigantlet hills nestled over the east. The south with its grand homes didn't have a mountain, so they created parklands and tree lined streets for their own little piece of nature. But no park or footpath, elm, beech or oak could ever replace the feeling of climbing to the nose of the Cavehill. Napoleon's Nose, as it was lovingly called for its resemblance to this famous general's profile.

Breathing in the fresh air as it rolled off the Lagan, my childhood eyes stood in wonder as fluffy clouds threaded and weaved into the earth through a thick blue line of sea. Standing near the edge, my dad would give me a geography lesson better than that from any book. Circumnavigating our piece of the globe he would point out the town of Larne shrouded in greyness. Its tall power station chimneys billowing and bellowing smoke into the cold north air. To its right, Carrickfergus nestled underneath its famous castle, looking more Lego like than majestic from our high vantage point. It had stood guard for many centuries over the mouth of the river protecting Belfast from Viking invasions. Now resting its laurels and canons it sleepily watched over the Heysham and Liverpool boats as they carried their passengers to new cities, new work, new lives. It also watched in 1912 the ill-fated Titanic sail through the narrow mouth of the river towards the wide Atlantic where she and 1500 souls would be consumed by the perils of the water she sailed on. Ahead Scotland could be seen hanging like a mist of silver blue across the horizon while far left the Sperrin Mountains and far right the Mourne Mountains separated our beautiful land into the man-made division of North and South. Below us dozed Belfast, a quiet city not yet torn apart by troubles. This was the mid-sixties; things were rumbling in the great White House on the hill, but as yet had not spilled over onto the streets below. Instead people spent their sharp frosty Sunday afternoons at firesides reading their Sunday papers or taking a nap in big old armchairs while digesting their Sunday roast.

But my dad had a different view of time well spent. Rain or shine, coats were buttoned up, laces were tied and buckles were tightened onto his willing volunteers, ready to head out for our "short stretch of the legs". Now don't be fooled by this statement as it usually involved quite a few miles. My baby steps skipping up Harmony Hill, Carr's Glen or Ligoniel, the Cavehill being saved till my shoes got bigger. By then our four-legged friend Ros accompanied us up the muddy paths. Oh how I envied him, those extra two legs, as I struggled to keep my balance on the stony ground that slipped beneath my feet…

Now it is 2012 and all those feet are gone but mine. Cancer had not only taken Dad's legs, it had now taken his life. I have been left to walk to my own drumbeat… But I couldn't hear it, I was lost. I had stumbled through the past year without a map or a compass. Lost and tearful under trees up the Cavehill. Lost in his greenhouse, squatting amongst his tomato plants. Lost in his garden shed, sniffing his wellies. If I'd been in there sniffing terps, I wouldn't have acted any more crazy. I was falling apart, but I knew that no amount of substance abuse was going to help me through this. I needed his strong hand to lift me.

In life he would never let you give up. As a toddler, if I fell, he would pick me up and take my hand in his; falling from my bike, he would sit me back on and hold the saddle; going under water swimming, he would cup my chin to keep me afloat. More recently, when I lay down under my duvet too tired to take any more chemotherapy for my own breast cancer, he called to hold me up. His strong secure hand was always there for me, from the moment he cupped my tiny toddler's chin in his palm (as his *'Little Pony'*) to last June, in his hospital room, when I lifted a now weak fragile hand to cup my chin in its warmth for the last time. When I gently returned his hand to the bed, I knew, as silent teardrops fell alongside it, that I had said my last goodbye.

Summer 2011 came and went. Christmas 2011 came and went. New Year's Day 2012 came and went. Easter 2012 came and went. Now I'm just 6 weeks away from June 24th. The first anniversary of the day my dad left us to travel to a cancer-free world. No tubes, no bags, no morphine; a place he could now walk once more with strong legs, his short stretch of the legs. But without his blackthorn stick… It is now neatly packed with my rucksack and, as he had once held my hand, I will now hold his blackthorn, and every step taken beside it will be for him and for those who had lost their fight against cancer.

2

Peep Toes and Pounding Pavement

April 27th. So, do I have a plan? No. My plan is not to have a plan. Clumping most of my annual leave together I have a Ryanair ticket booked to Biarritz for 30th May, and an Aer Lingus ticket is booked home from Santiago for 26th June. Anything else in between is a blank canvas. No sat nav or map just flecha amarilla (yellow arrows) and shell signs as my guide. I don't know where I will stop. I don't know where I will eat. I don't even know where I will sleep, but I do know that I will stand on the cobbles outside the Santiago de Compostela Cathedral on the 24th June. 500 miles to cover in 24 days, so this calls for some preparation. Well, actually, 23 days, as the 24th day I need to be in Santiago, so, by quick calculation aided by iPhone calculator, I needed to cover 21.739 miles every day. Not quite a 'short stretch', but, hopefully, manageable. Training for this was going to be difficult as I was working up to the evening of the 29th leaving only weekends and evenings to clock up the miles.

April, one would think, would be good for such training. Springtime, longer days, warmer sunshine… But Irish weather often meant hitting the Cavehill in winter woollies. In from work and suitably booted and layered, I would hit the paths round Belfast Castle at the foot of the hill for an eight mile trek. The route was a 1,5 mile circuit, so I was often dizzy by the sixth lap, but getting cheered on by the security men helped as I passed their hut over and over and over again. Struggling to reach eight miles, quitting at six, I began panicking that 21.739 was well beyond my reach. So, with positivity waning and night falling over me and North Belfast, my weary feet would plod home to repeat it all again the following evening. Weekends were much better. I would reach the top of the hill encouraged on by my chum Bernadette, who, rain or shine, struggled up beside me.

A big plus on these walks was my iPod music humming into my left ear. For whatever reason, my right ear was not the shape to accommodate said ear piece; instead, dangling in front, it muffled the bass notes into my scarf. Diana Ross's *Chain Reaction* covered the miles fast, Rocky's theme tune virtually had me running, but Hurts and Adele slowed me to a snail's pace. Often I could be heard singing along (badly) to these tunes as I clocked the miles into darkness. Singing is not a talent I inherited from anyone.

In need of more boppy tunes to cover the entire 500 miles, I dispatched this small instrument of technology to my baby son Conor to update, otherwise I'd be crawling up the Pyrenees while the plane was departing the runway in Santiago with one empty seat, mine. I had bought a new iPhone to take on the previous half Camino in September as it could multitask; pictures, songs and contact with home. Not to be. It spent 7 of my 10 days flat, courtesy of the wrong plug for its charger… I purchased what I thought was a European adaptor in Dublin airport, but no amount of hammering was going to get those two prongs into the tiny wall plug. Maybe, if I was in New York, it would have worked perfectly, as I had been sold an American plug!

Now, having ticked those two important boxes – training and music – it was time to think of the more practical things, like packing. A rucksack was a must, but a small one – an even bigger must. Max, my friend, had loaned me a rucksack, but it could have doubled up as a tent, so it got relegated into 3rd position. 2nd position was taken out from under my son Paul's bed. Dust blown from it and Thailand airport stickers removed, it was a strong contender. Smaller than Max's it had the potential to be my wardrobe for 24 days. But could I really carry a wardrobe for that period?.. Questionable.

So I went in search of "1st contender" rucksack. I was told by a patient that Millets were having a closing down sale. Perfect! I hoped to find a reduced rucksack not only in size but in price. I left the shop the new owner of a bum bag. Too late, I had missed all the bargains, but was reassured to try their city centre branch. So, car parked, I keenly sought out its sister shop only to be greeted by six pairs of size 14 boots and a few mosquito nets... Empty shelves screamed "too late!" at me as I left empty handed, but not without instruction to try their competitor across the street. So, while most girls spend their Saturday mornings trying on shoes, I spent mine trying on rucksacks in a very well stocked, if not overpriced, section of the shop. I had started downstairs where the prices were also down, only to be told these reasonable little items wouldn't see me over the Mourne Mountains.

So up I went to where serious people went to buy serious outdoor equipment. Four flights up similar to its prices, I rummaged through rows and rows of stock seeking out my purchase by colour rather than by effectiveness. This was soon knocked into touch by a very competent experienced salesman. I think I left with the Ferrari of the rucksack world in my plastic bag having been precision fitted to this item. Straps tightened and loosened. Too big, too small, too heavy, too light… Two hours later we finally got it just right. Well, everything but the colour… Purple is my least favourite colour. But the salesman was quite confident that after my first 100 miles with this little osprey on my back I wouldn't care if it was pink, yellow or candy-striped. Point taken, I headed for home.

May 1st. Training worthy of a military operation was going well; miles were being clocked up hourly, daily, weekly. I was on target for the end of the month when suddenly there was a problem… Coming down the hill I felt a chill around my foot. Looking down, I could see a tiny painted baby toe peeking out through the material of my Asics trainers. Possibly a pretty sight when accompanied by its fellow manicured toes in a pair of dainty summer sandals or peep toe shoes, but this was a warning of imminent disaster. These little size $3^{1}/_{2}$'s that had trekked me through the red soil of Africa, had nearly drown with me in the Mekong river of Asia, had pounded Belfast streets training for my 7 mile marathon, had tramped the Galicia mountain range and had climbed my legs to McArt's Fort, snow, rain or storm, were now breathing their last. Bought three years earlier, luminous white with their bright red strip, they proudly adorned my feet as I crossed the marathon finish line in Ormeau Park. In early April 2009 I had cobbled together five less enthusiastic chums to make up a Habitat for Humanity relay team. On the day, Max opted to be the driver, picking up and delivering us five runners to our handover points.. Hardly great, considering he was probably the youngest male on the team, but everyone was glad to climb into his warm car at the 'signing over' sections soaked through from heavy Belfast May Day showers. For years I had watched and applauded all those runners as they struggled up the Antrim Road near my home, promising myself that one day my feet would be of the footpath and on that road. Now that time had come. A Habitat fundraiser was the perfect excuse to tick that box.

Jogging was never my strong point, with January to May spent plodding the wet pavements of Belfast. My first attempt ended in a major stitch before I had even reached the top of my street, along with a strong desire to chuck up my dinner… Empty stomach now became a must for the remainder of training. New to my feet, these Asics settled in well. They lightly lifted my feet with their cushioned soles and wrapped around my ankles without as much as a red mark for their trouble. By May Day they had me ready.

As soon as I slid my feet inside them, I could feel their urgency to get going. Rain and wind didn't delay their determination as they helped me jog past my gang and my mum who excitedly jumped out from the crowd to hug me. I was signed up for the four mile leg falling in after Colleen, my friend who had run the East Belfast section. Handing over to Dermot at Lanark Way, I decided to keep going for another two miles as the route would pass my home, but I advised him and his fresh legs to run ahead while I made my way slightly slower to the pillars of Fortwilliam Park. By now my feet hurt, my legs ached and I was completely drenched through, so it was great to see Ciara, my daughter, cheering me on the last few yards. I had nearly made it home, and I could almost smell the bacon and sausage. Just as my taste buds were tingling at these thoughts, my mobile rang in my jogger pocket. It was my brother Stephen, he was standing with his boys about a mile further up the road waiting to cheer on their daft auntie. Another mile? I wasn't sure I had it in me, but somehow my legs and Asics rummaged together enough energy to jog past, smile, wave, look back and, when they could no longer see me, dart down a side street... I'd done it! I'd completed my 7 mile marathon! Max then gathered the team to run the last half mile beside Caoimhe, the last in our relay team. Not strictly allowed, methinks, but we had worked in Mozambique as a Habitat team, we ran the Belfast Marathon as a team, now we would cross the finish line as a team. Then we tucked into my daughter Aisling's big fry-up as a team round my kitchen table.

Later that day I laughed when my dad recounted how he missed me three times. First at the handover point when he was busy trying to find a better vantage point than the one my mum had secured. Then at Cliftonville Circus only to be turned back by police and stewards, and, finally, at the North Circular junction he waited only to be told by Stephen that I had finished. My dad never did see me run my mini marathon, but I knew he was proud of me.

Well broken in from jogging the streets of Belfast, rather than languish under the bed, a few weeks later these Asics found themselves packed ready to walk once more the wards of Leratong Hospice, a place built by my brother a few years earlier. This was my third trip to work and live in Atteridgeville, the township of Pretoria, and if there was one thing I had learnt from the previous three long haul flights, it was not to wear lace up boots when travelling if pudding feet were to be avoided. Trainers are a much more suitable option as my swollen feet could grow and spill over the sides with ease. But even before our plane left the ground they were a good decision when Paul (my son), Sean (a good friend from Sligo), Aisling and I covered what felt like the outskirts of London, never mind Heathrow, trying to get from terminal 1 to 4 at 2 a.m. having followed the directions of a well-informed foreign airport cleaner.

Once in Africa, these small trainers became an important part of my nurse's uniform. August baltic in this part of the world, I would start my 7 a.m. shift wearing a shirt, sweatshirt, coat, long trousers, two pairs of socks, my Asics and even a pair of gloves. Walking in them though was a rare event as I was too busy working double shifts 7 a.m.-7 p.m. every day and, unlike the previous three trips, walking outside the hospice perimeter fence was now too dangerous for our white skin. Around us the township had grown, but, like anywhere else, as populations grow, so does trouble. Combine poverty and homelessness together and you have a volatile cocktail. My brother had been shot in the hospice for a mobile phone two years earlier. Nothing different to poverty on the U.K. streets, but here we tended to stand out from the crowd. So any outings were always accompanied by staff that could vouch for our skin tone.

On one such expedition I did get a chance to walk to a party in the township. A lively affair catering for at least a thousand mouths. Food in large pots, we filled our plates with pap and stew, but only Paul and Sean braved the "walkie-talkies", a township delicacy of boiled chicken heads and feet. Aisling and I couldn't get past the hard toenails. Another day we walked miles through a safari park, giraffes and zebras strolling beside us in their natural habitat, but we thought it best to climb back inside the jeep to watch the king of the jungle. A majestic creature with an impressive mane, he walked with an air of great importance past our car towards a pry of lionesses all vying his attention. Though I do think a few of them were vying us instead for their next meal.

This visit was very challenging as I was left in charge of the hospice for the second week, though I did notice a big improvement in the control of AIDS since I first worked here in 2006. People were much better at taking their ARV medications and attending the clinic for blood tests. Now more a chronic illness than a death sentence, those that did die often did so due to a lack of good compliance with their treatments or else they chose to follow bizarre African folk remedies. While we were there we heard a baby had been raped by nine men as they believed this would cure them of the disease. Many young girls fell foul to this belief, contracting AIDS from a male family member for the same reason.

Three years had seen a big shift; beds were now filled by people in need of short term respite care and a nutritious diet. Only two patients died compared to eleven during my previous visit. Education was starting to have an impact; local self-help groups were now holding meetings in the hospice day care rooms. People were now standing up and saying *"I have AIDS"*, no longer frightened of community repercussions. One gentleman told me he had been banished to the hills outside his village as ignorance had created fear. Now his aim was to encourage people to step out from behind this stigma and seek help while they were still in the early stages. How to change beliefs he thought may take much longer and he feared the young girls of Africa may still pay a heavy price.

Two stressful weeks later the six nursing sisters returned, and I willingly handed over my control along with their DDA drugs cupboard keys. The hospice was still in one piece, but I was completely knackered and ready for home. Waved off by all the staff singing traditional African songs I knew my Asics were ready for the green grass of home. I took them on two more expeditions after Africa. A Habitat for Humanity Build to Chiang Mai in November 2009, when they rotated with my work boots, and in September 2011 to walk their first 200 miles of the Camino.

Late August 2011 they sat beside my hiking boots on the bedroom floor. I just couldn't make my mind up, which would be better for the job. Even whilst being driven to Dublin airport by Aisling, they both sat on the back seat of her car. Pulling up at the drop off section, a decision had to be made. I couldn't take both due to weight, so standing out on the footpath I deliberated for a few minutes then my mind was made up. My boots sat on Aisling's passenger seat back to Belfast.

This half Camino began at the end. I arrived in Santiago airport and had to bus it back to where I would start walking. Again, not sure of the Camino trail, I based my decision on the first bus to leave the station. Burgos or Leon? Hardly scientific or knowledgeable, but within an hour the bus left for Leon and I was on it. When I was disembarking into a cold dark Astorga at 2.30 a.m., I was beginning to doubt my choice. Stranded cold and tired outside a gated bus station, I fell in with two German girls who had befallen the same plight as me. The three of us had no choice but to bed down in the bus station doorway till the 7 a.m. connecting bus arrived for Leon as Astorga had failed to stay awake for our arrival. Albergues and hotels slept quietly on street corners, their large wooden doors tightly closed to passing trade such as ourselves. We did manage to find a café owner who took pity on us and poured us three coffees as the chairs were being stacked around our bar stools. When the mop was under our feet, we knew it was time to return to our doorway.

By 6.30 a.m. I had a great respect for the homeless. The ground was cold and unforgiving against my spine and the chilly night wind blew up my jeans. I found myself snuggling into two complete strange girls as we tried to create body heat. One lit a candle in her water bottle, and although this did little to improve our blood temperature, at least our giggles kept our faces from freezing over. Staring into its flame and feeling like the little match girl, I was beginning to question what had possessed a person of my age to undertake such madness. While most of my peers wouldn't drop below 4 stars on a hotel plaque, here was I, sleeping in the open under a million stars. Beautiful, magical, mystical and also – freezing in this Spanish autumnal night, but this was my choice. Others who frequented such doorways here and at home were not so fortunate. I would eventually be rolling up my sleeping bag and leaving my temporary accommodation for soft beds and fluffy pillows, but their bed would remain the hard cold ground.

Falling asleep with strangers, I woke with two new friends. Clambering onto the bus, slightly dishevelled from our experience, we all took a double seat and curled up on the itchy material for an hour's kip before we reached the city of Leon where our Camino would begin. I spent four fun filled days walking with my new companions before one succumbed to her blisters and I had to leave them as time was not on my side, but with promises of meeting once more on the Santiago cobbles. Now confident in my own company, my Asics and I meandered in and out of a large Italian group. Many had travelled solo like myself but found solidarity in their fellow countrymen. I learned so much from these wonderful people about their country, their culture and by Santiago I even knew a few Italian phrases. I was now an honorary Irish Italian spending most evenings delighting in the warmth of their company over pilgrim culinary delights washed down by carafes of red wine. Five days later hugged by Antonio at Santiago's bus station I climbed on board the airport bus for home in the knowledge that if I ever reached his Mediterranean shores I wouldn't need to seek out any cold doorways.

Now, eight months on from that 200 miles adventure, these same Asics are too tired to tread the Camino once more. Too weary for a charity shop, too smelly for a recycle bin, my old friends are ready to be put out to pasture, looking nothing like they had three years earlier. Their white now a dull grey, their red strip virtually invisible, and now a baby toe peeking through, but what an adventure they had taken my feet on.

Reflecting on their colourful past, I couldn't bring myself to bin them, so tucking them neatly under my bed with a heavy heart I sought out their worthy replacement, the new young Asics. Though the first week in May I soon discover is not a good time for such a purchase, all stock having been snapped up by keen marathon runners for Mondays Bank Holiday Run. Had I added my two feet together, I had numerous choices in size seven, but two feet in one shoe not practical for walking 500 miles, I resign myself on the advice of the sales assistant "to go online".

May 5th. Today I eagerly take the parcel from the postman and rip through the grey plastic packaging and bubble wrap till I reach the box. A sense of guilt overwhelms me as I excitedly opened the lid, knowing my old friends are lying redundant under my bed. I peek in… Gelled up, pumped up, brightly stripped, ready to carry my feet over 500 miles of Spanish terrain, but… not again! They were purple… Well, purple finish, but still – purple, my least favourite colour. First my rucksack, now my trainers, there must be a message in all of this?

So, laptop once more at the ready, I typed "purple" into the search bar.

A colour of good judgement.

A colour for persons seeking spirituality.

A colour for meditation.

A colour for peace.

A colour symbolizing mystery.

It will help re-balance your life, remove obstacles, calm over-activity and help you use your imagination to its fullest.

Thursday colour… Purple! The day I leave!

OK, I was in. Paint me purple and let's get going. I was going to embrace this colour. This was going to be my purple pilgrimage. Though I'm not sure even purple could remove the obstacle called the Pyrenees from my journey. But, as we take each step, we will always spare a thought for their predecessors. Red Asics are dead… Long live purple Asics. Now, to find the 'Compeed' plasters for the Irish blisters, I will acquire breaking in these bad boys before the 30th.

May 10th. My practice this week has a combined total of 18 miles in 4 days. Not a great effort, considering in 20 days I need to walk 20-22 miles daily for 24 days. My sums just aren't adding up. At this rate I reckon I should be home for Christmas dinner. I could blame the fact I'm working most days, and it's difficult to seek motivation when I get home. I could blame the fact that it's the coldest May on record and possibly the wettest. I could blame my new Asics for hurting, which they aren't. But really I can only blame myself. Going out in three layers of warm clothing wishing I'd brought gloves as the Irish winds and rain exfoliate my face or curling up on the couch in my large PJs and fluffy socks while demolishing a large bar of "Galaxy" as I watch *'Eat Pray Love'*… Well, really there is no contest as I tear away the gold coloured paper.

Maybe, if I put on *'The Way'* movie, it might kick my ass up the hill. But an independent Julia Roberts is hard to beat, and, I suppose, I could brush up on my Italian in the 'Eat' section of the movie. Brush up on my meditation skills in the 'Pray' section and brush up on my romance as I melt into the 'Love' section. Though all that melted (as Julia sails into the sunset) are the remains of my bar of "Galaxy", as I forgot I was sitting on it… So, to quote another fine actress Vivien Leigh as Mary Scarlett O'Hara, "*Tomorrow is another day*"!

I scrap the chocolate of the couch and my PJs and head to bed full of great plans once again not to make a plan as it would only be doomed to failure...

3

Puppy Fat and Posters

Another aspect of practice required is that of the native tongue. One thing I discovered from my shortened Camino last year was my lack of Spanish. To say my O-level Spanish is rusty is giving rust a bad name. I never could roll my tongue around those sweet sounding Spanish verbs. Personally I blame my lisp. A feature carried from childhood when my overactive tongue would get caught smack between my two front teeth and spray gentle words over the listening ear. An attractive lisp, a 'slight lisp', people would say, but, nonetheless, a lisp which now was causing havoc in my mouth as I tried to roll my tongue into a Spanish curl while clenching my teeth. Trying to say "Como esta?" with an Irish lisp just wasn't cutting it. But I needed to persevere if I was to pass myself; I couldn't walk the walk without talking the talk. Each bite into my tongue, I questioned – why I didn't listen better in language classes... More leaning towards English, History and Domestic Science, I would let my mind wander out to the lawns and rhododendrons that filled my Spanish class window in junior school and by 4th and 5th year that same mind had crossed the road to the boys' school nearby and my latest crush. Like my Spanish, I can't even remember most of their names. Like my lessons, I had a lot of crushes, and, like my lessons, most of them came to nothing. My biggest unrequited crush at the tender age of 11 was lavished onto David Cassidy, the Justin Bieber of the 70s. You were either a 'Donny girl' or a 'David girl'. I was a 100% 'David girl', my bedroom walls were living proof of this adoration. A 6 ft tall poster (bigger than the gent himself, I later found out), – all long hair, big eyes and fluffy white mid-calf boots. Today his furry flat footwear seems hideous, but I loved every last inch of that poster, not to mention the million other pictures of him that adorned my entire bedroom wall. However, my shrine to my first love was not appreciated by my big sister, who shared the room with me. Sharing a wardrobe and floor space was as far as it went. She was more into Leonard Cohen, possibly a musical and poetic genius, but not quite the pin up to have as your first crush.

Back at my school desk I knew David was slightly out of my reach, so my mind would wander past the lower sixth and upper sixth prefect's corridor, past the kitchens and their stomach churning smells of boiled cabbage and stewed meats, past the heavy scary convent door which hid the feetless ladies. In first year I feared that, if I went through that door, I would never come out, and for the rest of my life I would be forced to wear a habit and smell of rose soap. I never wanted a calling. I had many sleepless nights hiding under my blankets praying not to be called. But my mind, stronger than me, confidently slipped past the cream- and black-garbed ladies unnoticed, until it reached the tall gates of Dominican College, where it made its escape across the Antrim Road to the more available fourth and fifth years in the nearby colleges. Spanish verbs getting lost in my daydreams, the resulting outcome it was the only O-level I failed to make the grade. Languages were very much my weak point, and no matter how much my friend Mary tried to help me with homework, my brain just didn't function beyond our English speaking shores.

Mary and I had been together since P2, sharing a desk for the next fourteen years. In P7 we ran the tuck shop for our head mistress Mother Bernadette, eating most of her profits in the form of pink sickly shells, toffee chews and gobstoppers. Still chewing or sucking back in class a half hour later, our first employment created dental havoc to our back molars, a mouthful of mercury now living proof of our freebies. In Form 1 we ran the Scooby-Doo club making up food and toy hampers to be donated to poor families with small children at Christmas. In Form 2 we organized a sponsored walk to Corr's Corner and back. On a typical wet Irish Sunday we gathered a good crowd and also a few pounds for Africa. In Form 3 our rebellion arrived in a very mild form. Leaving school premises was against the rules, but we would run the gauntlet for an oversized cream torpedo from the nearby bakery. The dusty icing sugar ingrained on green gabardine usually giving us away back in the school yard…

Our second rebellion was to apply Maggie's mascara to naked eyes behind St Catherine's. Maggie was our hero. A true rebel, she smoked, she wore make-up and she wore a crombie coat rather than the shapeless bottle green 'Dexter' thing the rest of us hung above our indoor shoes in the cloakroom. While the teachers taught us what we had to know, Maggie taught us what we wanted to know. Mary and I were in awe. Following her exploits was better than reading last week's edition of the 'Jackie' magazine and much more informative. She knew the boys, she knew the places to hang out, and she knew everything. Mary and I had no chance of ever going there. Both on strict curfews from our parents, we left puppy fat and puberty behind, arriving into Rivita crisp bread and mascara laden adolescence on Maggie's coat tail.

In Form 4, back on track from our mini revolt and in a different class from Maggie, avoiding detention or suspension for our mutiny, we organized another sponsored charity walk, but this time to Tollymore Forest Park, in the heart of the Mournes. This though was not as selfless as our previous endeavours as it involved inviting boys from the local schools. Two Ulster buses hired and packed to full capacity, Bay City Rollers crackling on a tape deck, we headed into the East and a nine mile romantically charged hike. Shang-a-Lang wasn't required for the journey home as the rebel songs in newly broken male tones carried up from the back of the bus, with the front female passengers joining in the chorus. Those in the middle seats were too busy cuddling to care.

By Form 5 it was time to get serious and settle into the books as we helped each other study, Mary using her language and mathematical strengths, me using my literary, cooking and sewing skills. Doing well enough to secure our place on the senior corridor in lower sixth, we set about organizing our last joint venture the all-important school formal in The Europa Hotel. The most bombed hotel in Europe, it remained intact long enough to cater for our final big event before ours paths would divide, mine to the nurse's home and hers to teaching college.

Looking back though, it was our extracurricular activities that created the best school day memories. Our daily 3 mile walks down the Antrim Road to a bus stop at Carlisle Circus. This had a threefold benefit. It passed three boys' schools, we saved bus money towards the ceilis and discos, and we could both share the same bus stop home. Mary's bus taking her right back up the road we had just walked down. Seems crazy now, but when you're fifteen it seemed the perfect solution. Friendship, fitness and romance all in one. We thought the same, we looked the same, we even dressed the same, but luckily our taste in boys differed as we never fell out over a boy. Come to think of it, we never fell out over anything during our fourteen year friendship. We were always there to encourage each other's new love and pick up the pieces when it fell apart. Love was very capricious in our teenage world, we would spend weeks plotting how to meet boys and even longer figuring out how to get rid of them.

School terms were spent joined at the hip and summer holidays weren't much different. As two innocent fourteen year olds, we were dispatched to the Derry train at York Street station to spend three weeks at the Gaelteach. This was an Irish summer school in the hills of Donegal set up to take young teenagers from the troubled streets and cities of the north. Young lads who would be out rioting were instead packed off to the Christian brothers in Gweedore, the draw of young girls from neighbouring schools being a big pull. I remember all our parents waving us off happy in the knowledge that we would be well out of harm's way and that there was no way harm would come to us if the brothers had anything to do with it.

A strict regime, the brothers and teachers controlled the schools by day, while the *bean an ti* controlled the homes by night. Mary and I were in a house of about 24 girls sharing bunk beds in big dormitory style rooms. The *bean an ti*, her husband, her sister and their guard dog keeping a watchful eye. No young boy with rampant hormones would get within arm's reach of us, and, to make doubly sure, they were housed in similar prison-like accommodation up the hill. Even the ceili dances happened under the watchful eye of the men in cloth, but this didn't deter many a romance from forming on their shift. Paddy and I being one such couple. We fell for each other instantly, or should I say, we fell on top of each other instantly, the Belfast train throwing us together minutes after jolting out of the station. We were inseparable from that moment. Every morning he would make his way from the boys' house up the hill to meet me at the girls' house down the hill, and we would walk to school together. He was two years older than me, so he was in a different class, but every break and lunchtime we would spend it together.

Unless sport was on, then I knew I had to take second place to the Gaelic pitch. He was very athletic and played for both the Gaelic and the hurling team, so I spent quite a lot of time cheering from the sidelines. When his team won the finals, he gave me his winner's medal, so I think freezing on the line was worth it. Other free time would be spent on Bun an Inbhir beach or walking around the nearby lake, every fourteen year olds' fairy tale, puppy love and not a parent in sight. Hand holding and kissing the limit back in the halcyon days of the early 70s, but it was enough to stare into Paddy's coal coloured eyes and melt.

Only a few couples lasted the distance. Paddy and I didn't part until the train pulled back into York Street when parents picked up puffy-eyed daughters and maybe even the odd puffy-eyed son. Unlike me, Mary had only a few romances during the three weeks as she was carrying a torch for someone at home, so less inclined to fall in puppy love. Her eyes were much less puffy than mine, and her Irish was word-perfect. Arriving home, we embarked on the anorexic phase of our life. My mum blaming this on my dad calling us two little barrels when he saw us literally roll off the train having lived on bread, rhubarb jam and numerous packets of Mikado for three weeks. It was crisp bread and scale checks the rest of the summer.

A few years ago sadly I heard that Paddy had died, so, when I visited Donegal last year, I sought out our lake and set a little posy of white flowers on the still water for the handsome boy with black eyes. As I watched the flowers float out across the lake, I knew, Paddy would always be here. The sixteen year old Belfast boy, his black brogues clicking on the Donegal ground as we walked hand in hand.

My Irish is no better than my Spanish, and I never returned to the Gaelteach, opting for England instead. Here I could speak the language. On my second visit Mary joined me. We went for two weeks and came back after eight. The holiday money saved from our Saturday job in British Home Stores disappeared after the first week. Considering we only earned five pounds for our eight hour shift, one couldn't expect financial longevity. Luckily, we were staying with my cousin and her husband, but feeding and watering two extra mouths was more than enough. By now we had abandoned our anorexic diet in favour of the 'C' diet – if we saw it, we ate it – so the odd phone call was made home to tap our beloved dads for our social fund. Coffers replenished, we hit the disco scene of middle England with its flashing lights and sunken floors, mod cons that had not quite reached our world back home. We would rock the night away to *Rock the Boat* while blue fluorescent lights filled our mouths with whiter than white teeth. By our second visit we knew not to wear white bras for the same reason!

Another thing that had not reached our shores was the black taxi. The ones we knew ran on the Shankill Road and Falls Road to replace the buses that refused to run these volatile routes in the 70s, as a bus would make an excellent burning barricade. For a few pennies these public black hackney cabs would pick up passengers to bursting capacity while prams and shopping trolleys hung out from the boot. Here in England though you stood at a private taxi rank and your journey was metered. Not always a good thing when Mary and I hit a lean week. We would watch as that little clock ate the entire contents of our purses and we still had three miles to go. Taxied as far as our pennies would take us, the remaining walk gave us plenty of time to dissect our evening.

We worked as a pair knowing there would be safety in numbers. But it was a pain when it was your turn 'to take the mate'. We never found two mates we both liked, but that's what friends are for… Taking the mate! Eight holiday weeks in the fickle teenage heart is long and Mary and I broke and mended ours many times over with love and heartache. There is something masochistic about falling in and out of infatuation. Thankfully we never suffered the pain at the same time as that would have been too much for my poor cousin and her husband to bear. During the worst days of the pain we would play her weepy Motown LPs until she wanted to bin them. Cured, we would giggle with her into the small hours, lying on her purple shag pile carpet, backs propped against white leatherette couches talking about the new loves we had met in The George the night before.

One such love followed me home. Tony from Somerset. One blissful inseparable week together, our hearts broke as we parted at the train station, 'Sailing' by Rod Stewart deepening our agony. Vowing to keep in touch, his letters winged their way into my letter box every Thursday. First they would drop into my hall at home and then be tucked into my nursing home pigeon hole by amused wardens. These brightly coloured envelopes and pages covered in kisses would soon cover my bed. Read and reread until its replacement the following Thursday. When he passed his driving test, when he gave up smoking, when he got hammered playing football – I knew it all, but in the 70s it was much easier to get letters than people across the Irish Sea. Distance shores, distance relationships, distance grew, our letters stopping as we both turned our attention to less distant home waters… Earlier this year and thirty five years later, I found these faded letters at the bottom of my memory box when I was frantically searching for letters my dad had sent me to Donegal and England. My sadness suddenly lifted as once more these kiss covered pages were laid out on my bed and I giggled at the sweet innocence of teenage love.

Like Tony and I, after this holiday Mary and I started to grow apart; the 'Siamese twins', nick named by teachers in junior school, were to be no more. Time and life getting in the way as we both established our careers and new married lives, so it was with great amusement eight years later we found ourselves sharing labour pains as we both gave birth to beautiful daughters two hours and only a curtain apart. The new generation 'Siamese twins' were born.

But none of these memories were helping me to perfect my Spanish. Daydreaming 2012 style or daydreaming 1970s style still wasn't going to help me order a cup of coffee in the Basque region. So, back to my little Spanish phrase book for inspiration…

4

Hugs on the Hill

May 20th. Today I'm three feet from the edge of Napoleon's Nose and I'm sitting in contemplative mood on this big piece of basaltic stone that is wrapping itself around Belfast in a big stone hug. The hill that in 1795 Wolfe Tone, Henry Joy McCracken and other United Irishmen met to assert the Independence of Ireland prior to the 1798 rebellion. The hill that in 1899 saw Maud Gonne and William Butler Yeats climb in preference to the Giant's Causeway. The hill that kept Belfast folks safe when the Blitz burnt their city during the German air raids of April and May 1941 leaving devastation below. And, more recently, the hill that watched over a broken divided land as my childhood and the 60's drew to a close.

By 1969 the Belfast hills were no longer a safe haven. Wrong hill, wrong area and wrong religion were a cocktail for disaster. The halcyon days had gone and were being replaced by the gun, the bomb, the barricade and the bin lid on our streets. The air filled with fire and sulphur, the Cavehill, Black Mountain and Divis were now hugging a sick city. A city filled with bitterness and hate. I remember how I would lay in bed, the red flickering mast light unable to comfort my dreams anymore. A ten year old petrified into the mattress, heart racing in time with the ricochet of gunfire as mothers and sisters banged tin on ground to warn their men folk of imminent danger. The foot of the Cavehill had erupted into a war that would last almost 30 years. Families all scarred in some way. Mothers burying sons hardly old enough to shave, burying husbands still in their youth… The black widows of Belfast not quite into their thirtieth year. Graveyards shared in death by the murdered and the murderer… Men who couldn't share above the ground now rested side by side, below it.

We were luckier than most during this tragic period. My parents had a summer house on the edge of Dundrum bay, so, safely packed up and packed off, the beaches of Rossglass now became our walking ground. Slieve Donard peaks being kept for the more arduous treks. Summers and weekends of the 70's were spent swimming in the cold Irish sea, helping local farmers bring in the hay and cooking midnight BBQs huddled round embers of burnt driftwood on the beach. Happily in the County of Down, I walked my way through my teens. Only 37 miles away from everything that was wrong with our country, here I strolled through everything that was right. One summer's day even Gaelteach Paddy walked these country roads to surprise me. I was picking peas in my dad's vegetable patch in my wellies and dudes, so I wasn't impressed with the surprise. Well, maybe secretly I was.

Here we were safe; safe from attacks because of our religion, safe from my six brothers being drawn into any illegal organization, safe from any stray bullets. But we weren't! Our parents couldn't protect us from the hatred that now seeped like a weeping sore out from the cities. Its infection spreading through countryside at a speed no medicine could control.

A balmy August night 1977, home for the weekend from my abode, on the 13th floor of the nurse's home. Ten of us piled into two cars and headed to a disco in the local hotel. Music good and the fun even better, we were almost the last to leave the car park, not helped by my car being blocked in by another car. Finally in convoy we headed out the long hotel drive only to be caught in a massive explosion. A huge IRA bomb planted under the hotel oil drum caught both cars full impact. Daylight arrived for a few seconds as its brightness lit the sky. My car lifting from the ground heated like an oven before returning to the ground with an almighty thud. Opening its red hot door handles I quickly got everyone out before looking over my shoulder to an inferno. My friend's car was ablaze as raining oil fell from the sky like fireballs over our heads. *"Put me out, Carol Ann, put me out!!!"* His voice ringing through the stillness of the night sky… My two friends were stumbling towards me ablaze from head to foot. I was just a rookie nurse; numbly I took my leather jacket off and tried to beat out their burning flesh, rolling them up as best as I could on the ground to extinguish the flames. Nothing I had learnt in class or on my first wards prepared me for this. I felt hopeless and helpless as all around my world filled with burning friends, young frightened brothers, screaming cousins and burning cars. I was the oldest, I needed to hold it together for the other nine. Adulthood was thrust upon my eighteen years as I tried to keep calm amidst this living hell. I didn't want to be the grown up, I wanted someone else to take charge, but on that dark August balmy night there was no one else for what felt like an eternity until blue lights from the roofs of ambulances and police cars blinded my vision.

I fell to my knees beside my disfigured friends, their skin, hair and clothes smouldering, the smell of burnt flesh filling my nostrils. An ambulance man handed me my leather jacket as they gently lifted the two stretchers of the ground. Scorched and smelling, I wrapped it around my shivering shaking body in the hope it would hold me together as I still needed to drive the fourteen miles to the nearest hospital behind their flashing lights. I don't know how I got there, on that warm balmy dark August night. I don't know how I made it through the beautiful mountains of Mourne that sweep down to the sea. Met in the casualty waiting room by all our anxious parents, I handed my adulthood over to the real adults, as I curled up numb and cold on hard waiting room chairs, a very frightened eighteen year old, to wait and wait and wait…

My friends spent the next four years of their life growing skin to replace burnt skin. While I travelled up and down on my Honda 90 motorbike after nursing shifts for evening visiting time consumed with guilt. If we had left earlier, if I had not been blocked in, if I had not changed cars, if I had been better at first aid... So many 'ifs' I couldn't put right. At eighteen I had felt the full force of the Troubles, maybe not on the outside, like my brave friends, but sometimes our Troubles left invisible scars. The dead of our war will always be remembered, but those maimed and damaged, both outside and inside, will fail to be mentioned when history recalls "the Troubles".

Meanwhile my dad walked his way through our civil strife. When strikes, buses and barricades closed our roads, he walked the footpaths to work. When Belfast burned, he climbed his hills. Troubles didn't stop him heading out through the black days of the 70's with his black dog and his black thorn stick. Hatred suffocating our beautiful land into the 80's and 90's, he continued his walks, but this time in the company of a new mad red setter Ruairi, a big dopey dog that would lose himself once outside the gate. God hadn't given Ruairi a dog satnav like the rest of his pedigree, or, if he had, it had possibly been beaten out of him by his previous owner who had left him with a broken jaw and a mouth full of upside down teeth, a factor that scared every child in the district, including my own. For many years my parents didn't get their post or parcels as Ruairi's menacing appearance kept most postmen outside the gate. Walking past him unprepared was done at your peril, as his two front paws would greet you shoulder high, sending you flying into the nearby rose bushes. My daughter Ciara was unforgiving for many years after he tossed her three year old frame over his back into the front garden.

Ruairi arrived into the family via the Dog Pound where my brother took pity on him while seeking out a worthy replacement for our beloved Ros, who had given in to old age a few months earlier. Mad as a Hatter, from the day he entered our lives Ruairi was unbiddable on city walks and on Belfast hills, unable to heel at my dad's leg. Instead walks were spent on the beaches near the cottage, though quite often my dad could be seen leaping over cow pats chasing Ruairi who in turn was chasing the cows in nearby fields.

Ros had come from Rossglass, hence the great originally of his name invented by us seven children (baby brother Michael was yet to be born). Ruairi on the other hand must have come from space as he had no sense of anything on earth. I think he was slightly brain damaged from his earlier abuse, but nonetheless he became the eleventh member of our family for many years. And for many years my dad would spend many nights searching the yellow coated dolmens of County Down trying to find our Red King, the only dog in Northern Ireland without a sense of direction.

Succumbing to cancer in old age and having to be put down, my parents decided against another fur coated member for the family. By now the eight of us were busy being busy. I was either pregnant, pushing prams or doing night shifts in the casualty unit, so striding out with my dad became less and less frequent. My mum not a keen walker, her short stretch meaning exactly that, waved him off as they agreed to differ. So now, minus any two or four legged companions, my dad took to walking alone.

Though one tradition we always kept was Boxing Day. My favourite walk of the year began when I was a child; every Boxing Day we would trek to my grandmother's in east Belfast. Following the over indulgence of the previous day, those of us willing to brave the cold and join my dad would hop up in our new woolly hats and gloves and take to the quiet streets of North Belfast. Christmas trees would guide our way as they twinkled proudly from every window while the dark navy sky had its very own twinkling lights above our head. The air sharp against our cheeks made our noses drip onto new scarfs while eyes stung as frost cut between our lids, making our pupils glisten in the moonlight. My maternal granny lived across the river. This journey east was normally a two bus affair from our home. At one time the trolleybuses attached like Martians to overhead cables and underground tracks covered this route, but now open ended buses crossed the bridge which joined the east to the rest of my world. A world my dad walked when we were nothing but twinkles in his eye, when he travelled east to court my mum. I dare say their walks from the Club Orchid to her front door were very romantic short stretches of the legs over the dark river Lagan.

Technically, this narrow stretch of river separated County Antrim from County Down, so, by the time Dad and some of us twinkles had made it over the Albert Bridge, we were in a different part of Ireland. Though we were only 10 minutes from the heart of the city centre, it took us a good hour to come in from the north. The first three miles of our journey would walk us past garden fronts ranging from window boxes to Kew gardens, then past the large empty flax mills with their high porthole windows.

At one time half of Belfast's working population were employed in its linen industry, the north of the city being home to numerous mills, but these were now redundant, their looms silent, their pouce settled. Not the case though as we stepped off the bridge into the industrial east. A district that had grown up around its shipyard, docklands and aircraft industry. Houses tightly built in terrace rows to accommodate its workforce of at one time 20,000 men. Though few from my granny's district would be on its payroll, as she lived in the Catholic enclave known as 'Short Strand'. Probably taking its name from the piece of Lagan strand, running parallel to its road, from which a maze of numerous streets ran. While up in North Belfast we slept under McArt's Fort and the Black Mountain, my granny slept under Samson and Goliath, the large bright yellow cranes in Harland & Wolff, which dominated the east's skyline. Further out the road leading to the town of Newtownards, the houses surrounding the big white house 'Stormont' were quite palatial, but this was not a district familiar to my childhood. Our legs stopped just a few yards short of the bridge as my granny lived in the first street.

A corner site, it was home to my granny, my two uncles, my aunt and their children, so, with us ten invading on a Boxing Night, it left it packed to full capacity.. New dolls' prams, new bikes and pogo sticks filled the hall, while the kitchen table got cleared of Prof. Plum and Miss Scarlet before we could decide who killed Col. Mustard in the study with a dagger, or before you could buy

Mayfair or Park Lane. Left with Old Kent Road and a 'get out of jail' card, the all-important stuffing took centre stage on the table with loads of other tasty eats. My dad and my uncle were as close as brothers, laughing over pints in the local pub or packing up cars for road trips, but this friendship ended every Boxing Night over two plates of stuffing. Woe betide you sided with East over North, even if some years you preferred it. Later after much debate, deliberation and many more tasty mouthfuls, it usually ended in a sage stuffing truce, washed down by fresh Guinness or cream soda, in our case. Food cleared, games resumed, we made ourselves sick on selection boxes and tins of 'Quality Street' while waiting on the sing song. Christmas songs, funny songs, sad songs and the all-important Irish songs; a few of us showing off our Irish dancing "sevens" in the middle of an already packed room, trying to avoid knocking over the Christmas tree in our enthusiasm.

This chaos spilt throughout my granny's entire house every Boxing Night, but this was nothing compare to the mayhem that befell it when my English cousins arrived off the summer boat in their psychedelic miniskirts and high back combed hair. When this invasion hit from the other side of the Irish Sea, my granny must have thought that another Blitz had rained down on Short Strand, gas masks required for all the hairspray and perfume that would choke the air. I use to delight in visiting with my mum when they were in residence. I would watch in awe as they applied thick black liner above each eye with Picasso precision while waiting on rollered hair to dry from the heat of the parlour fire. I was only five, but I loved dressing up in their shoes and dresses and clanking around the house like a little mini Mary Quant. Friday or Saturday, when they were all trying to get ready at the same time for their big night out, it turned into a pantomime of powder puff and pancake sticks.

My granny was in her late 70s, and my mum was the youngest of her big family. Granny was born before the turn of the century into a Victorian era, when young ladies created wasp like waists from corset accessories worthy of a Harland and Wolff invention, and wore hemlines touching the ground, only rising above the ankle in the 20's. My cousins' hemlines touching the gussets of their American tan tights must have left her eyebrows as high as their dresses.

I loved visits to my granny and my Uncle Jack who always found three pence or on a good day a sixpence in his pocket for me and my big sister to spend at the corner shop. 'Andy's' wasn't as colourful a shop as my grandfather's sweetshop in the city centre. While my paternal grandpop's shop was an array of glass sweetie bottles, Andy had the more practical items of sugar, flour and porridge on his shelves. Everything seemed to be wrapped in brown paper, even Andy himself, towering way above my five years in his long brown overall.

Fresh Belfast baps, soda bread farls and floury bannocks sat on top of the counter in a wooden baker's tray while sweets were relegated to a small section in the corner, so spending my sixpence never led to making big choices to go inside my brown paper bag. But for my granny the most important thing in this shop was the phone hanging up on the wall to the side of the counter. Here every Saturday she would go down to wait on a phone call from my Uncle Jim in England. She was always very happy after this call.

My Uncle Jim and Aunt Sadie (my mum's older brother and sister) had moved to England many years earlier with their families to follow the work, leaving my granny heartbroken. Across the Irish Sea may as well have been across the

Atlantic Ocean in the 50's and 60's. It was very expensive to travel by sea or air in those days, so there was great excitement when the Irish invaded Britain for my eldest cousin Maeve's wedding. We all travelled on the overnight boat from North, East and West Belfast, but my granny, not liking the idea of sailing, took her first maiden flight into the air and off the green grass of Ireland. There was no way she was going to miss her first granddaughter's wedding. After this there was no stopping her as granddaughter after granddaughter and grandson got married. She was in every wedding picture right up front, with a new hat and a big smile. I remember at one of these events she told me to sleep on my piece of wedding cake, and I would dream about my husband. One week later changing my bed I found a mouldy piece of cake stuck to the sheet and a mouldy stain that wouldn't wash out. A sign that didn't bode well for my future. Most times though it wasn't wedding cake that flew back and forward over the waves, but soda bread, potato bread and malt loaf. Every time she or anyone packed to visit my aunt, half their case was filled with Kennedys or Hughes delights. Even when I went as a teenager, a few of these loaves had to be secreted between my disco dresses, a fact I wasn't too impressed about, mouldy cake memories still lingering in my brain. A mouldy disco dress certainly wouldn't find me the man of my dreams.

Walks to my granny's were the reserve of Boxing Day. Throughout the rest of the year this journey was taken on two buses, first with my mum, and, as we got older, my big sister and I were trusted to make this weekly journey on our own, to join our cousins for swimming classes in Templemore baths. An old building, cold tiling on the walls and even colder tiling in the pool. I remember standing at the shallow end with my rubber ring perched on the frill of my costume, while my sister and cousins swam like fish up and down the icy water. My skin was blue, but it was more from the air than ever from the water. Coaxed by Sally the instructor to join them, I usually got my costume damp just as the bell went, and we had to make it back to the little half door box cubicles that lined either side of the pool. If you had the misfortune of your clothes falling on the floor, as so often happened when three or four squeezed in, I usually went for my pastie and chips wetter than in my swimming gear.

Swimming never was my forte. If I couldn't feel *terra firma* beneath my feet, I panicked. So, my lessons came to nothing in Templemore, but I did learn a bit from my dad and his older sister, my aunt Marion. You had no chance of drowning when she took you swimming as the flowers on the bathing caps she made my big sis and I wear would have kept the Titanic afloat, never mind a five and six year old. Losing us was never a problem as we were always easily spotted, looking like Esther Williams, with floating flowerpots on our heads. If this wasn't reason enough to report my wonderful aunt for child cruelty, a second reason was for her putting us into the freezing outdoor waters of Victoria Park, swimming a must if hypothermia was to be avoided. Though, all worth the abuse when our legs hung from tall stools in front of tall milk shake glasses. Pink milk to match pink flowery hats that now hid in pink wet towels below our pink feet.

Boxing Day walks east stopped many years ago, but we continued our tradition on the hills of North Belfast. Starting at the Horseshoe Bend, ending at McArt's Fort before heading home to nibble the turkey carcass, Dad's home-made stuffing and hot steamy drinks. For two years now I have been doing this walk alone. In 2010 I called to taste his stuffing, in 2011 my mum didn't quite make it the way he did, but she tried… He never did tell any of us his secret ingredient.

Now, as I sit on the edge of Cavehill, I can still see Victoria Park in the distance. Smiling, I wonder – could walkers see our bathing caps from up here all those years ago?.. My eyes scan over the east, the Mournes a blur 37 miles away, the newer shipyard cranes bright yellow in the sunlight, the narrow river Lagan, landfill bringing the North and East within touching. North Belfast sprawling below, the mills now modern apartment living, the rows of Ardoyne streets silent from the sound of the bullet and the bin lid, Dominican College, a state of the art building, unrecognisable from the old 'year houses' of my adolescence… Till through the trees my eyes come to rest on my dad's eco car, dormant in his driveway. It is almost one year since my heart broke into unfixable pieces. In 35 days I will reach the end of my Camino, but I will also reach the end of the saddest year of my life. So today, against the biting May winds, I tighten his gardening jacket around me and hug it tight while wishing he could be in it just once more. I close my eyes to hold back the tears, and then, as if from a whisper on the wind, I hear what he would say…

"Let's go for a short stretch of the legs".

Wiping my eyes, I lift myself to my feet and smile over his Belfast, knowing that in 10 days I will do exactly that.

5

Find a Penny, Pick it up

May 23rd. So far I'm ready to walk the walk and trying badly to talk the talk. But if I am going to be mad enough to walk 500 miles, I felt that someone should benefit from this lunacy. So I had a light bulb moment. "*A Penny Mile Camino*". On the streets a major recession was going on, so I couldn't very well ask people to dig too deep into their already empty pockets for sponsorship, but a penny for every mile I walk should be manageable. Setting a target of 1000 pounds for Friends of the Cancer Centre, all I needed was 200 people to donate a fiver. Less if the government gave me their 25% cut.

A phone call to the Cancer Centre, a Just Giving page set up, now all I had to do was share it on Facebook, Twitter and LinkedIn, and hope for the best. Meanwhile, for my part, I will take 500 pennies with me and every mile I walk I will leave a penny in memory of all those who have died from cancer and in thanks for those like myself who have survived this disease. My last penny I will keep for my dad and I will leave it in his memory at the crypt of St James in Santiago Cathedral.

"Find a penny, pick it up… for today you will have good luck".

I must be on a lucky streak. After rummaging through pockets, purses and piggy banks I found 459 of these little copper coins. 41 to find for my mission to be complete, I set about removing all the cushions from my couches. Four scrapped fingers, two hairclips, a broken pen, and one mouldy chip later, I was rewarded with 8p. The pound coin I found I put in my purse. Two days and 33p later, donated from a niece and a girl in work's purse, I wrap this heavy bundle tight in a plastic bag and tuck it deep in my rucksack. My Penny Mile Camino was ready to commence. Well, after I pack.

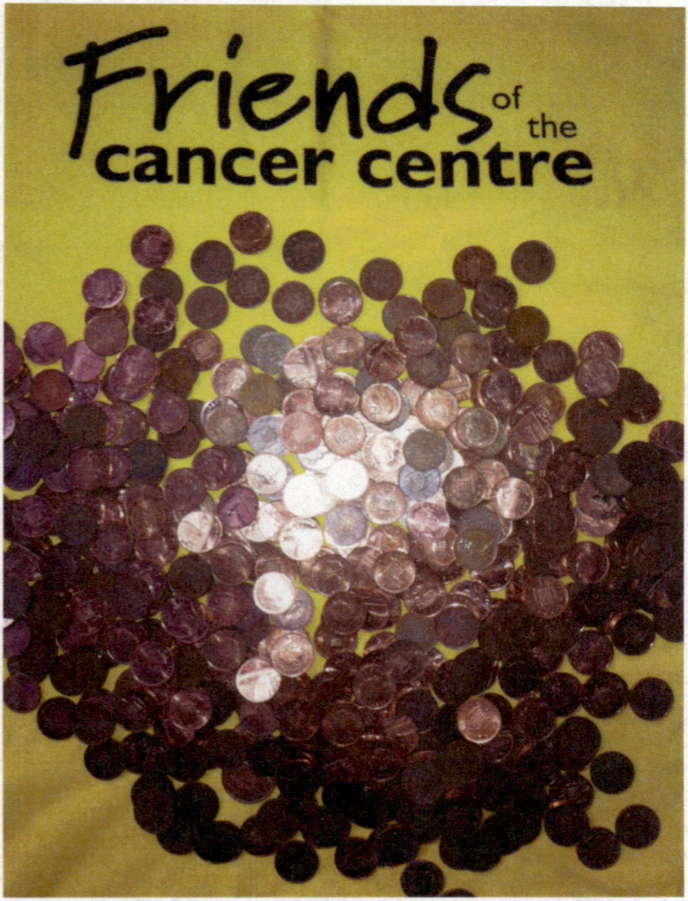

May 29th. Wednesday my last day at work finally arrived, referrals referred, notes noted, desk cleared, computer switched off I head for home to face a large bundle of clothes on my bedroom floor worthy of a Bear Grylls expedition. Keeping a check on the Spanish weather not a great help as it varied from 34 degrees in Burgos to 12 degrees with heavy rain in Galicia. Based on this information, the smallest North Face jacket I could purchase has been added to the pile.

Decisiveness was now called for. The back packers' guide to a happy rucksack is all in the weight. It must be 10% of your body weight. Stepping off my bathroom scales at 50 kg gives me 5 kg to play with. Not a lot, but then again vest tops and shorts are light. However, toiletries, sleeping bag, raincoat and shoes – aren't, and that's before I add water and food. Unable to be aggressive in my decision making, I enlist my daughter Aisling for a more cut throat approach. She was assigned the "*Don't need it – don't take it*" bundle, while I was assigned the "*Take that*" bundle. She won!

The pile on the bed behind her was massive, while my paltry pile looked quite lost beside my rucksack. I could have saved a lot of money on that little purple osprey as this lot would fit into my bum bag, and no amount of pleading with my daughter was going to get me a third pair of shorts. So my little "*Take that*" bundle, minus the lovely Gary, Mark, Howard and Jason, who resided in my iPod, was rolled up and squashed into my rucksack. My life for 24 days looked quite miserable. Then we set about bottling soap, shampoo and sun cream into bottles which would hardly cater for a weekend in Lilliput Land or Hobbitsville, let alone almost a month on the road. I was now feeling quite sorry for the person who would have the misfortune to be seated beside someone resembling